13 ESSENTIAL LESSONS

FOR YOUTH AGES

14-18

Conversational, experiential lessons reveal the heart of Jesus—and how teenagers can live out a relationship with him each day.

NO. 02

JESUS-CENTERED

100%

FROM THE

NEW TESTAMENT

13 Essential Lessons From the New Testament
© 2016

group.com
simplyyouthministry.com

Credits
Executive Developer: Tim Gilmour
Executive Editor: Rick Lawrence
Chief Creative Officer: Joani Schultz
Editor: Stephanie Martin
Art Director and Cover Art: Jeff Storm
Production: Suzi Jensen
Project Manager: Justin Boling

ISBN 978-1-4707-4451-9
10 9 8 7 6 5 4 3 2 1   21 20 19 18 17 16

Printed in the United States of America.

13 ESSENTIAL LESSONS FROM THE NEW TESTAMENT
TABLE OF CONTENTS

[X] EASILY REPRODUCIBLE

[X] OPEN-ENDED QUESTIONS

[X] FLEXIBLE FOR ANY SIZE GROUP

[X] WRITTEN USING THE NEW LIVING TRANSLATION

[X] ENGAGING ACTIVITIES

HOW TO USE THESE LESSONS...

This collection of *13 Essential Lessons From the New Testament* is a taste-test overview of crucial topics, threaded through a narrative that is always pointing forward to Jesus. The lessons are structured simply, using an "inquiry based" method that maximizes conversation and engagement with your teenagers. This question-focused structure gives you the flexibility to tailor these lessons to your time slot, and go as deep as your group is able to go. We believe healthy discussion is essential to help students own their faith. Even more, you don't have to be a theologian to lead these lessons. We've crafted them specifically to emphasize discussion and deeper connections among students. If you love God and love teenagers, you can easily lead these lessons.

Each lesson is built on Group's REAL teaching imperatives: Relational, Experiential, Applicable, and Learner-based. Each week, your kids will build relationships with each other, and with God, through interactive experiences and challenging questions that will spur them to dig deeper. And every lesson is threaded-through with a Jesus-centered focus that reveals and elevates the Messiah, no matter what the topic or scriptural foundation. In addition, we include ideas for connecting what kids are learning to their everyday lives with every lesson. The lecture (or "talk") strategy that so many use as a default setting has proven to be the least effective way for people—not just teenagers—to learn. In fact, more and more learning experts are now branding the talking-at-you method so popular in churches as "educational malpractice." With these lessons, you get a "best practice" approach that will plant growth in your students.

As an added resource, we've included a short "background" segment that will help you quickly get up to speed on the topic focus of each lesson. And we've included two suggested "Tweet-able" invitations you can send out to teenagers in advance of each lesson.

Now, just like that, you're ready to lead these lessons. Follow the flow from start to finish, or cherry-pick the lessons that fit your scope. We're so grateful you've picked up this resource, and honored to partner with you in your ministry to teenagers.

Grace,

Rick Lawrence
Editorial Director
Group/Simply Youth Ministry Resources

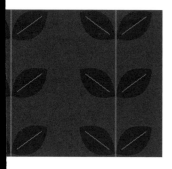

ACTIVITY

Say: **Imagine for a moment that one of your family members has disappeared. It's quite likely that everyone in your family would search everywhere and do whatever it took to find that person. In this clip from the movie *Cheaper By the Dozen*, the Baker family realizes that one of the children, Mark, is missing. The whole family begins to search for him, looking everywhere they can. Eventually they find him on a train headed to the city where their old home was located.**

Play the clip.

Ask:

- **How is this family's reaction similar to or different from the way your family would respond in this situation?**
- **Think back to when you were younger. How did it feel when you got lost or didn't know where your parents were?**
- **Who was responsible for finding you? How long did it take?**
- **What emotions did you experience after you were reunited with your family?**
- **Have you ever been the one who was searching for a lost person? If so, what happened?**
- **If Jesus is just like a shepherd searching for lost sheep (us!), how do we typically make it hard for him to "find" us?**

Say: **We may not like being compared to sheep, but the care our parents provide is similar to what shepherds do for their sheep. That's right—sometimes you're like sheep! We all are, in fact, according to the Bible.**

DIGGING IN

Have students take turns reading aloud Luke 15:1-7.

Say: **Let's explore what this relationship between a shepherd and a sheep looks like.**

Things you need...

- ☐ A video clip from *Cheaper By the Dozen*, from 1:20:45, as the family pours out of the house, to 1:23:45, as Tom and Mark hug
- ☐ An Internet connection and a computer or tablet to display the video
- ☐ Paper
- ☐ Pens or pencils

BIBLE BACKGROUND

Read Luke 15:1-7.

As a teacher, Jesus knew he could effectively connect with his audience by using familiar ideas and images—including sheep and shepherds. Most of us don't have much interaction with sheep these days, but it was a common occupation in Jesus' time, especially in Israel.

Sheep and shepherds were also central to the religious heritage of Jesus' audience, thanks to stories and characters from the Old Testament (the only part of the Bible written at that point). David was a shepherd boy long before he became king of Israel. Moses tended sheep for his father-in-law, Jethro. Before Rachel met and married Jacob, she was a shepherdess. Amos was a shepherd before God called him to be a prophet. So Jesus' listeners would have had some understanding of the role, importance, and dedication of a shepherd.

Sheep aren't always the easiest animals to lead. The key is helping them become familiar with their shepherd's voice. It's almost like a child's ability to recognize a parent's voice in a large crowd. Ultimately, a shepherd's job is to protect the sheep, take care of them, lead them to food and water—in short, do whatever they need to thrive.

THE SHEPHERD CARES

Ask:

- Why does Jesus describe himself as a shepherd?
- Why does the shepherd in the parable leave the 99 to find the one? What makes that one sheep so important?
- Think of a specific time when Jesus has acted like a shepherd in your life. How did Jesus care for you? What did you learn from that experience?

Say: **Jesus often describes himself as a shepherd, and sheep and shepherds appear many times in the Gospels. Just as a shepherd provides care for sheep, Jesus wants to take care of us. He wants us to know his voice and listen and obey; that way, he can guide us out of danger and lead us to "green pastures." Jesus meets our needs and knows what's best for us.**

THE SHEPHERD SEEKS

Ask:

- When have you experienced Jesus' love for you in an unmistakable way?
- In your life, how have you felt pursued by Jesus? Think of a time you felt kind of lost in life; what helped you feel "found"?
- Read Isaiah 53:6. Why do we leave God's paths to pursue our own?
- What are some consequences in your life if you choose to leave God's path?

Say: **When sheep get separated from their shepherd, they can feel alone and end up in trouble. The same is true in our relationship with Jesus. When we wander from him or ignore his voice, we feel alone and sometimes find ourselves in situations that aren't the best for us. When we read Isaiah 53:6, we can take comfort in knowing that Jesus loves us so deeply he'll do whatever it takes to find us when we're lost and then care for us as a shepherd lovingly cares for his sheep.**

DIGGING DEEPER

Ask:

- Think of a time when you experienced something you didn't necessarily like but that produced something positive in your life. How did you sense Jesus' involvement in that experience?
- When have you been frustrated in your relationship with Jesus? When has he seemed silent? What was that like?
- Sometimes we turn to "shepherds" we know aren't good for

us or who invite us into bad habits, instead of depending on "shepherds" who want the best for us. When have you turned to other "shepherds" besides Jesus to meet your needs, and why?

Have students form pairs. Give each pair paper and a pen or pencil.

Say: **With your partner, read Psalm 23. Identify and write down all the different shepherd tasks and images included in this Bible passage.**

After a few minutes, bring the group back together.

Ask:

- **What shepherd tasks and images did you find in these verses, and what's the spiritual significance of each?**
- **Why does David compare God to a shepherd?**
- **If David were writing this psalm today, what other character or analogy might he choose instead of describing God as a shepherd? Explain.**

PUTTING IT INTO PRACTICE

Ask:

- **What's the theme or big idea from this parable?**
- **What story from your life is similar to the story Jesus tells?**
- **This week, when you feel yourself getting anxious, pause and do something simple to remember your "Good Shepherd." Simply say, under your breath: "I'm just a sheep, and I need you Shepherd."**

THINGS TO REMEMBER

TEXTS & TWEETS

What do you have in common with sheep? See you soon to talk about it!

Feeling a little lost? Come hang out for some help in getting back on track.

Make texting your group easier. Consider using Simply Text. To try it FREE go to https://secure.symt.us/signup

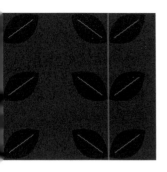

13 ESSENTIAL LESSONS FROM THE NEW TESTAMENT

LESSON

THE UNFORGIVING DEBTOR

No.02

BIBLE VERSES | **Matthew 18:21-35**
Luke 6:37

ACTIVITY

Share a story about your first memory of experiencing forgiveness. It probably happened when you were a small child and you got in trouble for doing something you shouldn't have. You experienced forgiveness (we hope!) from your parents.

While you're sharing the story, have a student make several stacks of pennies on a table or the floor—or you can do it as you're speaking. Make sure the stacks have unequal heights.

After you've told the story, ask students to, one by one, stand on a chair or somehow get directly above the stacks of pennies. Ask them to take note of the way the stacks look from above. Next, have them look at the stacks from the side, at eye level.

Say: **These different stacks illustrate different perspectives on our sin. When we look from the side, it's similar to our earthly perspective on sin. But when we look from above, it's similar to Jesus' perspective on sin.**

Ask:

- **Which sins do we tend to think of as being worse than others? Why?**
- **Which sins might Jesus say are worse than others, if any? Explain.**
- **How does this illustration help you re-frame the differences between our perspective on sin and Jesus' perspective on sin?**

Say: **Jesus, looking from "above," sees our sin and our need for grace and mercy. Even though each sin may have different consequences—a child lying about stealing from the cookie jar probably doesn't hurt anyone else, but a murder hurts an entire family and community—sin is sin and needs forgiveness. Today we'll talk about forgiveness by examining a parable Jesus tells when someone asks him about this topic.**

Things you need...

- ☐ Pennies (at least 10 per student)
- ☐ A backpack filled with heavy books

BIBLE BACKGROUND

Read Matthew 18:21-35.

Forgiveness in Jesus' culture came with a price. The Old Testament clearly outlined laws and guidelines for dealing with sin. Disobeying God's commands led to consequences. But by Jesus' day, some religious leaders had gone so far as to basically make it their full-time job to hunt down and punish sinners.

That was the context for the question Jesus was asked in Matthew 18:21. His audience probably expected some rules and regulations—when it was okay to punish someone else and when you had to show mercy. He shocked everyone by saying forgiveness has no end. No human is ever perfect, so no one has the right to tell someone else they don't deserve grace and forgiveness.

How you approach the subject of forgiveness depends on your teenagers and their specific life experiences. Some may want to forgive a bully for saying something mean at school or want forgiveness from a sibling for hogging the computer. However, some may be wrestling with how to forgive an abusive parent who's in jail or the person who killed a friend in a drunk-driving accident.

(continued on next page)

DIGGING IN

Have students take turns reading aloud Matthew 18:21-35.

Say: **Let's talk about some biblical truths about forgiving people—even when it's tough.**

LEARN TO FORGIVE OTHERS

Say: **When we accept Jesus' forgiveness—made possible by his death and resurrection—we are freed of a debt we could never repay. Yet we sometimes turn around and refuse to forgive other people of lesser debts. If we remember how much Jesus has forgiven us, we may be more than willing to forgive people who wrong us.**

Ask:

- **When have you had a similar experience to the man who needs forgiveness and approaches the king in this parable? What about that same man in the second half of the story; when have you been in a position to forgive someone but struggled to do so?**
- **Read Luke 6:37. What's the connection between our willingness to forgive others and our ability to receive forgiveness?**
- **For you, which is easier: receiving or giving forgiveness? Explain.**
- **When did you most recently forgive someone for something, even though it was hard?**

LEARN TO KEEP FORGIVING

Give everyone 10 pennies. Ask students to each make two piles: one representing their sins that need forgiveness and another representing the things they need to forgive others for.

Ask:

- **Why did you choose to divide your pennies this particular way?**
- **Think of one person you're having a tough time forgiving; why is that?**
- **Think of one person you might go to for forgiveness; how can you do that?**
- **What's easiest about forgiveness for you? What's hardest about it?**
- **Describe how you've grown in your willingness to forgive, or be forgiven.**

Say: **Forgiveness is a choice, and it takes time. You don't forgive someone and "get over it" instantly. Sometimes it's a process of repeating to yourself daily—hourly, if necessary—that you're** choosing to forgive someone. Young musicians practice scales so fingers are trained to play the right note. After repetition and time, it just comes naturally. The same is true of learning the habit of forgiveness. You may be at a place right now where you have a greater need for receiving forgiveness than giving forgiveness—or vice versa.

LEARN TO STOP COUNTING

Ask:

- How do you relate to Peter's question in Matthew 18:21? How have you handled friends or family members who seem to "sin against you" a lot?
- Why do we remember how often someone has committed a particular sin? Does that mean we haven't really forgiven that person? Why or why not?
- What kinds of "sins against you" might lead to the end of a friendship?
- What role does forgiveness play in friendships?
- Respond to this statement: It isn't possible to have a deep friendship without learning how to forgive.

Say: **Learning to forgive takes time and effort, but learning to forgive someone who sins against you repeatedly is even tougher. It helps to remember this parable from Matthew 18 and to realize how frequently we sin against Jesus—yet he continues to love and forgive us. Sometimes it may be best to end or suspend a friendship with someone who repeatedly betrays or attempts to manipulate us. And if another person is abusing us in any way, this verse should never be used as justification to remain silent.**

DIGGING DEEPER

Ask:

- **This parable has three main characters—who does each one represent, and how does this help you understand Jesus' message?** [The king is God, we have a large debt, and the co-workers are other people in our lives who need our forgiveness.]
- **In the parable, the man owes the king millions of dollars but the fellow servant owes the man a few thousand dollars. As best as possible, stack up the whole collection of pennies to represent the different amount of debt. How does this help you better understand the acts of forgiveness in this story?**
- **What's the difference between the king's perspective on debt— and the opportunity for forgiveness—and the man's perspective?**

You may have a hard time discussing forgiveness because you struggle to accept Jesus' grace for sins that seem too big to forgive or because you struggle to forgive someone who's hurt you deeply. Continue to pray through your own process of forgiveness, and use discernment in what might be encouraging and appropriate to share from your experience.

Say: **Forgiving ourselves can be just as hard. Guilt is a powerful tool that Satan uses to affect our walk with Jesus.**

Hold up a backpack filled with heavy books. Ask one student to put it on and try to do pushups while wearing it. Although that might be possible, it's difficult.

Ask:

- **How have you felt sin "weighing you down" in your life in the past? How have you felt it today?**

Next, have the same student try doing pushups without the backpack. It will be much easier.

Ask:

- **Jesus' forgiveness is supposed to give us freedom; how do we experience that freedom?**
- **How have guilt and shame weighed down your relationships with other people?**
- **What's one way you can move toward experiencing freedom from a lack of forgiveness in your friendships and family relationships?**

PUTTING IT INTO PRACTICE

Ask:

- **What's the theme or big idea from this parable?**
- **What story from your life is similar to the story Jesus tells?**
- **What's something you can receive Jesus' forgiveness for right now?**

THINGS TO REMEMBER

LESSON

THE TEN BRIDESMAIDS

N⁰·03

BIBLE VERSES **Matthew 25:1-13**   Philippians 3:12-14
          1 Corinthians 9:24-27   2 Timothy 2:5

ACTIVITY

Things you need...

None

Say: **Think about a major event or commitment in your life and what it takes to get ready and prepare for that experience. Maybe it's a recital or a final exam or the biggest game of the season.**

Ask:

- **What "big" moment comes to mind, and what kinds of emotions do you experience as you think about it?**
- **What role does your attitude play in your process of preparation? Do you feel a strong sense of anticipation? excitement? expectation? Explain.**
- **If someone has a negative or pessimistic attitude, how does that affect the preparation process?**

Say: **When we get ready for a big event, it's important to have the right attitude. That's where it all begins. If you aren't hoping for a good grade, you won't study as effectively. If you don't expect to win the game or succeed at a recital, you won't practice as hard. Once the right attitude is there, then the details become important!**

Ask:

- **What are some specific steps you take to prepare for a big event?**
- **In the past, what's happened when you took shortcuts or didn't invest the time you needed to get ready?**

Say: **This lesson challenges us to live daily for Jesus, honoring and loving him in all we do. It also encourages us to live in a way that shows we're meant for more than our time on earth. Jesus talks about himself as a bridegroom to the church. His role is to unconditionally love the bride, the church. The bride is invited and called to love and trust Jesus. Preparing for a big event, competition, or celebration can be fun; preparing for eternity with Jesus is even more meaningful. God created us to love and worship Jesus in heaven for all eternity, and as Christians, he calls us to live in a way that reflects our faith in Jesus right now.**

BIBLE BACKGROUND

Read Matthew 25:1-13.

Jesus wants us to understand the importance of being prepared for his eventual return. When you read through Matthew 24, you see that he's prophesying about future events. Jesus' thoughts and theme continue into chapter 25, including this parable.

Ten bridesmaids take their lamps and go to meet the bridegroom, but he doesn't arrive as quickly as everyone expects. Only five bridesmaids are wise enough to bring along extra oil for their lamps. When the five "foolish" ones realize they're out of oil, they ask the other five for some but are denied. The five foolish bridesmaids leave to find more oil, and while they're gone, the bridegroom returns. Only the five wise bridesmaids are allowed to enter the wedding feast. The five foolish ones eventually come back but aren't permitted inside.

The parable's final verse reveals the challenge Jesus is putting before his followers: "So you, too, must keep watch! For you do not know the day or hour of my return" (Matthew 25:13). Jesus says we must be prepared and ready for his return. We don't know when it will happen, but we need to live our lives in a way that points people to him and eternity in heaven.

DIGGING IN

Have students take turns reading aloud Matthew 25:1-13.

Say: **Let's look at what it means to be prepared for Jesus' return.**

KNOW WHAT'S AHEAD

Say: **The best way to prepare for the future is to be aware of what Jesus says will happen. As we read through the New Testament, we discover numerous reminders and promises of Jesus' return. Here in Matthew 25, Jesus clearly tells his disciples that he will someday return—although he doesn't say exactly when it will happen.**

Ask:

- **As you read this parable, which of the characters do you most relate to, and why?**
- **In Matthew 25:13, Jesus says we don't know the day or hour of his return. Why doesn't God tell us the exact day Jesus will return? What impact might that knowledge—and lack of knowledge—have on the way we live?**

GET READY

Say: **You have lots of choices. You can choose what clothes to wear, where to sit on the bus, what people to greet in between classes, who to talk to at lunch, how to spend your free time, what sports to play, and so on. Jesus challenges us as Christians to use our time wisely. In this parable, he tells his disciples to "keep watch."**

Ask:

- **What do you think Jesus means when he tells his disciples to "keep watch" and await his return? In real-life terms, what does this mean?**
- **What's one specific way your choices right now are helping to prepare you for eternity in heaven?**
- **How do the entertainment media you consume—movies, TV, video games—affect your faith? How does your faith affect what you choose to see and do?**
- **It seems harsh that the "foolish" bridesmaids are left out of the wedding party because they didn't prepare well. How does this punishment fit the "crime," in your mind?**

BRING ALONG OTHERS

Ask:

- **How does your knowledge of Jesus' eventual return affect the** way you interact with people who haven't yet decided to follow Jesus, if at all?

Say: **If you know that Jesus will someday return *and* that you have the opportunity to spend eternity in heaven with him, you have the chance to tell your friends. Look at it this way: If you know something that can positively change a friend's life, why wouldn't you share that knowledge or information? Friends desire the best for each other, and that includes wanting them to experience a meaningful life now and an eternal life later because of Jesus.**

DIGGING DEEPER

Say: **As a teenager, you might feel like most of your life has nothing to do with church or Jesus, but think about it in terms of sports. If you went to practice for an hour a week but then ate an unhealthy diet and never exercised outside of that official practice time, what kind of athlete would you be? Like any "all-in" pursuit in life, our life as a follower of Jesus is an all-the-time relationship.**

Ask:

- **Read 1 Corinthians 9:24-27; Philippians 3:12-14; and 2 Timothy 2:5. How does an athlete practice self-control and self-discipline in the training process? Why are self-control and self-discipline important?**
- **How is living a life that honors Jesus similar to running a race or competing in a sport and receiving a prize?**
- **What's one "training habit" that has helped strengthen your relationship with Jesus?**
- **In what area of your life are you most challenged in living out your relationship with Jesus?**

PUTTING IT INTO PRACTICE

Ask:

- **What's the theme or big idea from this parable?**
- **What story from your life is similar to the story Jesus tells?**
- **Here's a simple physical thing you can do every morning, right after you get out of bed, to prepare yourself for a day with Jesus—silently, just open your arms for a few seconds to invite him into your day.**

TEXTS & TWEETS

If you were arrested for being a Christian, would there be enough evidence to convict you? Don't miss a fascinating topic.

What does it take to "get ready" for eternity with Jesus? Let's talk about it together.

Make texting your group easier. Consider using Simply Text. To try it FREE go to https://secure.symt.us/signup

THINGS TO REMEMBER

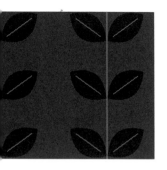

13 ESSENTIAL LESSONS FROM THE NEW TESTAMENT

LESSON

THE TALENTS

№-04

BIBLE VERSES

Matthew 25:14-30
Genesis 12:1-3

ACTIVITY

Share a story from your teenage years about a time your parents or a teacher got annoyed at you for wasting something. Perhaps you put little or no effort into something or wasted the opportunity to do something well or something at all. The idea is to help students realize that parents and teachers generally want us to work hard and do our best. These adults get frustrated only when we don't put much effort into something.

Ask:

- **What coach or teacher has had a positive influence on your life? How has this person helped shape who you are today?**
- **How do you respond when a coach or teacher pushes you to excel or reach a goal you think isn't possible? Why do you respond that way?**
- **How is the idea of excelling in athletics, arts, or academics similar to or different from excelling or growing as a follower of Jesus?**

Say: **Most teachers or coaches probably won't become world-famous, break Olympic records, or have their faces on the big screen. But the way they teach and coach with excellence can change lives. We've all been given resources—time, money, talents, skills, connections, passions, intelligence, relationships—that we can use to serve Jesus, bring him honor, and help other people.**

Say: **An incredibly talented and famous musician can bring Jesus glory by being the best musician in the world, but also by using those skills to invite people into worship. Someone who makes millions in investments may be the reason medical missionaries can afford to go serve people in other nations; it's the financial genius backing the venture. The most popular player on the soccer team can be intense and competitive on the field but be kind and inviting to opponents and respond with grace and patience when others are frustrated. The key is discovering what God has given us and then using those resources to bless him—and others.**

Things you need...

- ☐ Paper
- ☐ Pens or pencils
- ☐ Envelopes

BIBLE BACKGROUND

Read Matthew 25:14-30.

At first glance, the parable of the talents may seem unfair. The one person who doesn't take risks with the master's wealth actually does nothing to *lessen* it. He takes what he's given, protects it, and returns it in the original condition. He does nothing "bad," and nothing at all. But doing nothing is the problem.

This parable comes at an interesting time in Jesus' ministry, just before he's crucified. It's part of a two-chapter focus on the kingdom of heaven and Jesus' eventual return. Jesus is about to leave; in the parable, the manager is gone. We know Jesus often hinted about his departure, but his disciples don't seem to understand what he's saying. Later they grasp the significance of continuing Jesus' work. They're specifically called to do so in Acts 1, and in that book we see them mobilizing and changing the world for Jesus.

Because we use the New Living Translation, you'll see references to "silver" instead of "talents." A "talent" is simply a measure or weight of something. Money translates to blessings.

DIGGING IN

Have students take turns reading aloud Matthew 25:14-30.

Say: **Let's look at how you can use your God-given talents to faithfully honor Jesus through serving other people.**

DISCOVER YOUR TALENTS

Ask:

- **In this parable, Jesus uses money as the illustration to communicate his point. What are some other blessings, resources, and talents God has placed in your life? Be as specific as possible; sometimes it's hard to talk about our good qualities!**
- **Why do you think Jesus gives all of us talents and abilities?**
- **We can use our talents and abilities to do great things in the world, but Jesus doesn't need us to change the world. Why, then, do you think he wants us to move through our talents and abilities to further his mission?**
- **What does it mean to be faithful with your talents?**
- **Describe a time when you benefited from someone else's talents.**

Say: **You may not realize it, but you have time, opportunity, money, talent, material, education, technology, and many other resources at your fingertips. Jesus created the church to be a dynamic, living group of Christ-followers who each contribute something to the whole. And that doesn't just mean adults. You have something to contribute, too. Jesus needs your gifts and talents... today!**

SEARCH FOR OPPORTUNITIES

Say: **Jesus will place you in positions where you can serve, and he invites you to seize opportunities that come your way. As his disciples, we have the opportunity to use our spiritual gifts, passions, abilities, personalities, and experiences in ways that honor Jesus and draw people to him.**

Ask:

- **What's one way you've discovered you can bless others with your gifts and talents?**
- **If you could choose to serve Jesus in any capacity, what would you be doing? Why?**

SERVE FROM A DESIRE TO HONOR GOD

Say: **Gary Haugen is an example of someone who's found a way to honor Jesus through his gifts and talents. He used to work as a** lawyer at the U.S. Department of Justice and as a United Nations' investigator. He now leads International Justice Mission, an organization that works with officials around the world to free people from slavery and other forms of oppression. Gary's position and influence gave him the platform for starting this international organization, and now he helps save the lives of thousands, returning dignity and health to people who've lost their human rights.

Ask:

- What is at stake for Jesus in whether or not you give your best in school, on the field, on the stage, or at your part-time job?
- How does giving your best honor Jesus? How does not giving your best dishonor him?

Say: **You can impact your world for Jesus. We know that some parts of God's plan aren't yet fulfilled. Theologians use the idea of an "already/not yet kingdom." Jesus came and declared his kingdom, but he returned to heaven, promising that one day he'd return. So the key is discovering what you can do today to use your resources, skills, and talents for God's glory. Our time, talents, skills, passions, gifts, and resources are not our own. They're simply on loan from God with an expectation that we multiply them while we have them. And we wait for Jesus to someday tell us, "Well done, my good and faithful servant."**

DIGGING DEEPER

Ask:

- What's most surprising about the way the boss responds to each worker's investment in Matthew 25?
- Why might the boss respond to the third worker the way he does?

Say: **Pair up with another person and read Genesis 12:1-3. Then answer these questions together.**

Ask:

- Why does God bless Abram? What does God want him to do with his blessings?
- How have you been a blessing to others in your life? What's one step you can take this week to become a greater blessing to someone in your life?

Distribute paper, pens or pencils, and envelopes. Ask students to write themselves a letter detailing how they want to grow spiritually, emphasizing how they can use their gifts, talents, abilities, and resources to honor Jesus. Encourage them to write about the person

they hope to be in a month, at the start of next semester, in six months—whatever makes most sense for your group.

Explain that you'll mail the letters on the agreed-upon date, and no one will see what they've written. Allow about five minutes. When students are done writing, have them seal and address the envelopes to themselves. Make a note in your calendar to mail the letters as promised.

PUTTING IT INTO PRACTICE

Ask:
- **What's the theme or big idea from this parable?**
- **What story from your life is similar to the story Jesus tells?**
- **The next time you're practicing one of your gifts or talents, just whisper a "Thank you, Jesus" in the midst of it.**

THINGS TO REMEMBER

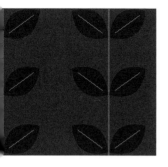

ACTIVITY

Give students each a 3x5 card and a pen or pencil.

Say: **Think about the most meaningful conversation you've had in the past few weeks. Maybe it was with a friend, a sibling, a parent, or a role model. On your card, write a few words that explain why that was a meaningful conversation. Then turn to a partner and share why the conversation had such an impact on you.**

Allow several minutes for discussion. Then bring everyone back together.

Ask:

- **Why do some conversations have a great impact on us, while others turn out forgettable and insignificant?**
- **If you could have a conversation with Jesus while sitting in the middle of your school cafeteria, what types of things would you want to talk about? Why?**

Say: **Jesus is good at having conversations that leave an impact on the people he encounters. His comments and questions are powerfully intentional, and people walk away changed—or at least challenged. Today we'll look at a passage that includes one of the most familiar verses in the Bible. We'll discover what Jesus says in that conversation, and how it impacts our lives today.**

DIGGING IN

Have students take turns reading aloud John 3:1-21.

Say: **Let's explore this Scripture and see what type of impact Jesus' words can have on our lives.**

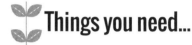
Things you need...

☐ 3x5 cards
☐ Pens or pencils

BIBLE BACKGROUND

Read John 3:1-21.

This Bible passage reveals a powerful conversation that leaves a lasting impact on one man's life—and it contains a verse that continues to impact lives today. Jesus' words about believing provide a foundation for what it means to have faith. Believing in Jesus affects how we live and how we interact with other people. Jesus came to offer light to a dark world in order to show God's love. Even though we're naturally drawn to the world's darkness, Jesus wants us to embrace his light. As we grow in faith, we have the opportunity to spread Jesus' light in a world filled with spiritual darkness.

John 3:16 is a well-known verse with theological depth: God loves the whole world, Jesus is God's Son, and believing in Jesus leads to eternal life. Every word in this verse reflects God's love and intentions to save humanity.

Jesus says we must be born again to be saved, and he chastises Nicodemus for being a spiritual teacher and not understanding this. It can be difficult to gain a new perspective; if it were easy, we'd find more open-minded people! We know we're not perfect, and we're looking for something more. Faith in Jesus—being born again in the Spirit—fulfills our deepest need. God loves us that much.

JESUS' WORDS IMPACT OUR THINKING

Ask:

- If you had a face-to-face encounter with Jesus, what questions would you want to ask him, and why?
- What's most surprising about Jesus' words to Nicodemus in verse 3? Why?
- What truths does Jesus reveal in this conversation? Which ones do you believe? Which ones are difficult to accept or leave you asking more questions?
- Jesus challenges Nicodemus' understanding of spiritual truths; how has he done the same thing in your life?
- How might you explain the phrase "born again" to someone who doesn't yet know Jesus?

Say: Jesus came to save us from a life of despair and an eternity separated from God. We must gain a new perspective, a new understanding of how God sees us—and what God requires of us. Nicodemus thinks he knows what it means to please God, but Jesus impacts his way of thinking. Jesus wants to have the same impact on your way of thinking. He wants to change how you think about the world, other people, your purpose in life, and how you can make a difference.

JESUS' WORDS IMPACT OUR PRIORITIES

Ask:

- If you've decided to follow Jesus, how is your life different because of it? How has putting your faith in Jesus impacted the way you live?
- Look at verses 18-21. Spiritually speaking, what is the darkest place you visit on a regular basis? Is it your school, your job, your neighborhood, or some other place? Why is it so dark spiritually?
- What are specific ways you're living out your faith today that give people a little "taste" of Jesus? How have you been a "light" pointing the way to him?
- How do these verses help you more clearly understand the way your actions, deeds, and attitudes impact your relationship with Jesus?

Say: Jesus uses nighttime as an illustration for the world. The world is living in darkness, but Jesus comes as the light to bring life. When we follow Jesus, he impacts our priorities—and those changes impact the people around us as we follow, love, honor, and obey him.

JESUS' WORDS HAVE A LASTING IMPACT

Ask:

- Why do you think so many people memorize John 3:16 but not John 3:17?
- How might your non-Christian friends respond to verse 16 if they also hear verse 17?
- Rephrase those two verses in your own words. What do you find most meaningful about them, and why?
- People often write "John 3:16" on big signs at sporting events and other public settings. How does that familiarity with John 3:16 affect the impact of Jesus' words on a 21st-century audience?
- How have you walked away different because you've truly spent time with Jesus?
- You can't sit down and talk with Jesus face to face, but you can still communicate with him. How have your conversations with Jesus affected your life?
- What tough questions have you asked Jesus lately? What answers has he given?

Say: **It's amazing that some 2,000 years after Jesus and Nicodemus speak, we continue to memorize and recite John 3:16. It's one of the most well-known verses in the Bible. But the next verse is so important because it reveals that Jesus' mission was to save, not to condemn. When we follow Jesus' example of love and sacrifice, his words continue to have a lasting impact on people's lives.**

DIGGING DEEPER

Ask:

- Overall, what's your takeaway from the conversation between Jesus and Nicodemus?
- When was the last time a friend asked you a spiritually focused question, like Nicodemus asked Jesus? What happened?
- Read John 7:50 and 19:39. What do these verses reveal about Nicodemus and the impact of his conversation with Jesus? How do these verses affect your perspective of Jesus?
- Read John 10:10. What does Jesus desire for your life? How have you begun to experience the life he's speaking about here?

PUTTING IT INTO PRACTICE

Ask:

- What are some specific ways you can "talk with Jesus" in the context of your everyday life?

TEXTS & TWEETS

How have Jesus' words impacted your life? Let's talk about that—and more.

How do your priorities reflect what matters most to Jesus? Get ready for some great conversation!

Make texting your group easier. Consider using Simply Text. To try it FREE go to https://secure.symt.us/signup

- How will you respond if a friend asks you to explain why you follow Jesus?
- What's one question about Jesus you won't know how to answer, if a friend asks you? How can you prepare yourself better to answer that question?

THINGS TO REMEMBER

LESSON

THE PARALYZED MAN LOWERED DOWN

N⁰·06

BIBLE VERSES **Mark 2:1-12**   Ephesians 4:1-6
Proverbs 14:29   2 Peter 1:2-7

ACTIVITY

Say: **When we experience a challenging situation, we face three options: (1) Do nothing, (2) make a negative impact by viscerally reacting, or (3) make a positive impact by thoughtfully responding with patience and love. A** *reaction* **is reflexive, fueled by emotion. We react according to how we feel. Reactions are often selfish and shortsighted. A** *response* **is thoughtful and non-anxious. We respond according to our ability to open ourselves to the Holy Spirit, appropriately impacting situations and honoring Jesus, our neighbors, and ourselves.**

Have students form two groups. Label one the Reactors and one the Responders.

Say: **Reactors, your actions should be reflexive and fueled by emotions. Responders, your actions should be thoughtful and non-anxious. After I read each note card, discuss the scenario for a few minutes in your group. Then you'll take turns role-playing your reaction or response.**

Repeat the process for all four situations. After the second scenario, have groups switch roles so they each have a chance to be Reactors and Responders.

Ask:

- **What was it like to be a Reactor? a Responder?**
- **Think of a time you reacted to a situation instead of responding. How might you have handled things differently in order to produce a different outcome?**
- **What must happen inside you to respond rather than react?**

Say: **The situations you just acted out are quite different from the situation in the Bible passage we'll discuss today. However, we'll be able to see how Jesus lovingly responds, rather than reacts. As we examine this Scripture, we'll consider some ways we can embrace Jesus-centered truths for our lives today.**

 Things you need...

☐ Four 3X5 cards that each contain a situational description. Use these ideas or create your own:

- Your friend leaves her smartphone at your house. Before you can stop him, your little brother starts playing with it and accidentally drops it in the toilet.

- You're playing in the soccer championship, and emotions are running high on both teams. In the last seconds, your star player is lined up to make the winning shot, but then an opponent swipes for the ball, taking your teammate out of the game.

- Your parents accuse you of doing something you didn't do.

- You're waiting at a red light and someone rear-ends your car—which, of course, actually belongs to your parents.

BIBLE BACKGROUND

Read Mark 2:1-12.

After returning home from days of travel, Jesus is surrounded by a crowd—likely in Peter's house. Though undoubtedly exhausted and deserving of rest and relaxation, Jesus extends grace to the crowd.

The paralyzed man's friends just know that if they can get to Jesus, their friend will be healed. The crowd prevents the friends and paralyzed man from entering the home by traditional means. Desperate, they decide to climb atop the dwelling and dig a hole through the roof to lower the man through it, to Jesus' feet.

Undoubtedly, debris falls to the floor. Imagine the disgust of the witnesses. Making a hole and lowering the man through the roof would've been quite the spectacle. The men destroy someone else's property! Despite all this, Jesus doesn't react with anger or offer a scolding. He sees the opportunity for what it is: a way to reward the faith of the friends who love the paralyzed man enough to get him to Jesus; a way to forgive the man's sins, healing him on a spiritual level; and a way to physically cure the man, demonstrating God's power and Jesus' authority.

DIGGING IN

Have students take turns reading aloud Mark 2:1-12.

Say: **Let's jump in and see what we can learn from these Bible verses about the impact Jesus' actions can have on our lives.**

JESUS' ACTIONS CAN HAVE AN IMPACT ON YOUR THINKING

Ask:

- **Tell about a time someone else's actions changed the way you thought about that person, about yourself, or about a situation. What was most significant about that experience?**
- **Lots of surprising things happen in this Scripture passage. What do you find most surprising—and why?**
- **When the paralyzed man is lowered down through the roof, what are some ways Jesus could have behaved differently toward the group?**
- **Why is it significant that Jesus forgives the man's sins before he physically heals him?**
- **In this passage, what idea or truth do you find most powerful about Jesus' actions, and why?**
- **How do your thoughts affect the way you act toward other people? Give a specific example, if possible.**
- **How is your thinking different because you follow Jesus? Be specific.**

Say: **Jesus very easily could have had the group of friends arrested for destroying the roof of that home. But that isn't how he chooses to respond. And instead of letting the Pharisees silently question his actions, Jesus confronts them and demonstrates his authority as the Son of Man by telling the paralyzed man to stand up and walk. Sometimes it's easy to think we know best, but Jesus' actions often contradict the way people think. Just as Jesus practiced patience and afforded grace, let's look for ways to pause and consult with him before responding.**

JESUS' ACTIONS CAN HAVE AN IMPACT ON YOUR BEHAVIOR

Ask:

- **Think of a time you weren't proud of how you reacted to a situation. How might things have gone differently if you had taken the time to respond rather than react?**
- **Share a story about a time when you or someone you know handled a situation by responding with patience and grace. What did you learn from that?**

- How have you learned to prepare yourself for difficult situations? Be as specific as possible.
- What are some examples of how practicing grace and patience can have a positive impact on others?

Say: **Jesus impacts us with his actions because they're often surprising. Not only does he heal the paralyzed man on a spiritual level by forgiving his sins, he also heals him physically, astonishing the crowd gathered there. When we read about how Jesus carried himself, it can remind us to continually invite him to guide our own responses to challenging situations in our lives.**

DIGGING DEEPER

Ask:

- **Read Ephesians 4:1-6. To what calling is the Apostle Paul referring?**
- **Look at verse 3. What does it mean to be united and bound together in peace? What does that look like, practically?**
- **Read 2 Peter 1:2-7. Peter identifies specific things we need in order to support our faith. Why are those things important?**
- **How can these verses help you prepare to be more of a responder than a reactor?**

PUTTING IT INTO PRACTICE

Ask:

- **What are the biggest hurdles or obstacles you face that prevent you from responding appropriately to certain situations?**
- **What are some specific things you've done to become more patient?**
- **We can control only our own actions, not those of other people. How has your own patience impacted others?**

TEXTS & TWEETS

Think of a time you did something that someone else thought was wrong. How were you treated? Come share the answer.

Do you sometimes struggle to practice patience and offer grace? Find a path to growth— and bring a friend, too.

Make texting your group easier. Consider using Simply Text. To try it FREE go to https://secure.symt.us/signup

THINGS TO REMEMBER

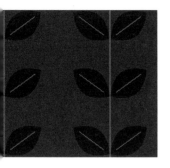

13 ESSENTIAL LESSONS FROM THE NEW TESTAMENT

LESSON
THE WOMAN AT THE WELL

Nº.07   BIBLE VERSES   **John 4:1-30, 39-42**   Matthew 28:16-20
Proverbs 18:21

ACTIVITY

Play the song.

Ask:

- **Which word or phrase from this song had the greatest impact on you, and why?**
- **What are some common ways teenagers seek satisfaction in their lives?**
- **What does it mean to be spiritually thirsty? How is that similar to and different from physical thirst?**

Say: **This song is rooted in a Bible passage we'll look at today: the story of how a woman drawing water at a well encounters Jesus, and how that "chance" meeting had a huge impact on the people in her town. A moment of impact with Jesus leads to a whole bunch of other moments of impact for the people in this woman's town. And you can have an impact on the people around you, too, as you share the message of Jesus.**

DIGGING IN

Have students take turns reading aloud John 4:1-30, 39-42.

Say: **Let's look at how sharing the message of Jesus can impact other people.**

ONE CONVERSATION CAN IMPACT SOMEONE'S LIFE

Ask:

- **Think about a recent conversation you'd describe as meaningful. You don't have to share details, but tell why the conversation was so meaningful or memorable.**
- **Based on your understanding of the Bible, what does the phrase "the message of Jesus" mean to you?**

Things you need...

☐ A lyric video for the Casting Crowns song "The Well": youtube.com/watch?v=JKioQPEW4do

☐ An Internet connection and a computer or tablet to display the video

BIBLE BACKGROUND

Read John 4:1-30, 39-42.

The Samaritan woman draws water from the well at noon, when she can avoid people's ridicule, speculation, and gossip due to her life circumstances. Suddenly, she finds herself engaged in conversation with Jesus. Though the conversation remains civil, the woman's tone maintains some skepticism and challenge, even after Jesus speaks of her many marriages. But as the conversation continues, the woman becomes more inquisitive.

When Jesus informs the woman that he is indeed the Messiah, she is shaken enough to leave behind her water jug—even though that's why she went to the well in the first place. Jesus' impact is so powerful that the woman must share the news that the Messiah is among them. And once her neighbors hear the message of Jesus, they experience life-changing impact, too.

One conversation with a Samaritan woman ultimately impacts many people because she can't stay quiet with the truth she's encountered. And because many hear the message, many come to know Jesus.

- Why is it vital that Jesus' followers share his message with other people?
- When you're in a conversation with someone, what evidence would they see in you to prove that you genuinely care? Explain.
- What qualities does Jesus demonstrate while he's conversing with the woman at the well?
- What do you find most surprising or unexpected about the conversation between the woman and Jesus? Why?
- Even though it was considered improper behavior for a man to be alone with a woman—let alone engage a woman in conversation—those cultural boundaries didn't dissuade Jesus. What are some modern-day cultural boundaries that might become barriers to having a Jesus-centered conversation? How can you overcome those barriers?

Say: **We're often presented with opportunities to share what we know with people who may have doubts or questions about life and faith. But when we engage people in conversation, we have the potential to impact them in many ways: We can help them understand something they don't know, we can help them work out something they are doubting, or we can just listen. As long as we maintain a non-anxious presence, we can invite the Holy Spirit to work through us to impact the other person in our conversation.**

SHARING YOUR STORY CAN LEAD OTHERS TO FOLLOW JESUS

Ask:

- We typically like to connect with others after we've experienced something amazing, fun, or life-changing—so why do we often feel self-conscious about sharing after we've experienced something amazing with Jesus?
- What adjectives—descriptive words—would you use to describe the woman's response to Jesus' declaration that he is the Messiah?
- Why might it be significant that the woman leaves behind her water jug?
- The woman chooses to go back to her town and share her story with the people there. What's the connection between bravery and faith, between boldness and being a follower of Jesus?
- Even though the woman is something of an outcast, she still spreads the message of Jesus. Talk about a time when you had something important to say but chose to remain quiet. What happened as a result?

Say: **Many people find it a little scary or intimidating to talk about their faith stories or share the message of Jesus with others.**

Sometimes, though, Jesus puts people in our path to work through us. The story of the woman at the well teaches many things: No matter the circumstance, it's a good thing to engage in conversation with people who are thirsty for truth. Once we learn an important truth, we need to find a way to share it. And like a wildfire, that truth will spread, impacting many, many more people.

DIGGING DEEPER

Ask:

- When has it felt most natural to have a Jesus-centered conversation with someone who isn't a Christian? Where is it most challenging to have that kind of conversation?
- Read Matthew 28:16-20. What do you think it means to "make disciples"? How can we do this in our world today?
- What statement in this Bible passage seems most helpful or encouraging, and why?
- Read Proverbs 18:21. How does this Bible verse relate to today's discussion?

PUTTING IT INTO PRACTICE

Ask:

- For you, what seems most difficult about sharing your faith with others?
- What are some important ideas to remember about the right and wrong ways to engage someone in a Jesus-centered conversation?
- Let's exchange stories of how Jesus has impacted our lives. In other words, why are we followers of Jesus, and what does Jesus mean to us?

Say: **When faced with a serious conversation, one way to prepare is to pray beforehand, asking the Holy Spirit to fill you and give you the right words to say. During the next week, consider committing to praying each day, asking Jesus for wisdom, patience, grace, and the right words—so when you do have important conversations, he'll empower you to make a great impact for him.**

TEXTS & TWEETS

We eagerly tell others when we've experienced something amazing, fun, or life-changing— like Jesus! Join us for an interesting conversation.

What do you think it means to be a disciple? Can't wait to see you soon.

Make texting your group easier. Consider using Simply Text. To try it FREE go to https://secure.symt.us/signup

THINGS TO REMEMBER

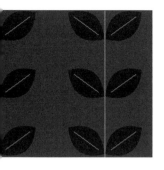

LESSON

THE RICH YOUNG RULER

N⁰.08

BIBLE VERSES

Matthew 28:16-30 James 2:14-26
Ephesians 2:8-10

ACTIVITY

Distribute paper and pens or pencils.

Say: **You'll have one minute to make a list of everything you own. The goal is to fill the page with as many things as possible in just 60 seconds.**

Tell students when they have 30 seconds left, and then 15 seconds. Call "time" when the minute is up.

Say: **Look at your list and cross out anything you'd consider a necessity. Then circle all the remaining things on your list that aren't "needs."**

Ask:

- **What made this activity difficult or easy?**
- **If someone told you to sell all your possessions so you could serve people through a religious organization, what emotions might you experience?**
- **What connection do you see between making sacrifices and growing as a follower of Jesus?**

Say: **This exercise helps us weigh the impact of Jesus' words to a rich young ruler who asked what more he needed to do to get into heaven. It also can help you understand the ways Jesus intends for us to impact our world in order to demonstrate his love to others.**

DIGGING IN

Have students take turns reading aloud Matthew 19:16-30.

Say: **Let's dig into this Bible passage to learn how our actions can impact our life in Christ.**

Things you need...

- ☐ Paper
- ☐ Pens or pencils
- ☐ A stopwatch (or some way to keep track of time)

BIBLE BACKGROUND

Read Matthew 28:16-30.

Is this Scripture about a man who can't give up his stuff? Is it about Jesus expecting us to be perfect? Or is there some meaning we can't easily grasp? Even theologians have difficulty answering these questions.

When discussing this Bible passage, many people focus on the rich man. But this lesson focuses mainly on what Jesus says after the rich young ruler leaves. Jesus explains that nothing we do can get us into heaven, but if we follow him and give things up for him, we'll receive eternal life.

In addition to the suggested opening activity, check out the "Rich Young Ruler" skit from The Skit Guys. It's a creative presentation with a poignant message. You can preview, buy, and download the skit at http://skitguys.com/videos/item/rich-young-ruler.

Jesus challenges us to leave everything behind and follow him. He wants us to let go of things we cling to; he wants us to live as servants, giving to people in need. Jesus taught us to serve as he serves, to love as he loves. And the impact of following him doesn't end with us. Once Jesus has impacted our lives, we'll affect the people and the world around us.

JESUS CHALLENGES YOU TO MAKE AN IMPACT THROUGH YOUR ACTIONS

Ask:

- What's most surprising to you about this Bible passage, and why?
- Why do you think Jesus would instruct the young man to sell all his possessions?
- Jesus says it's almost impossible for a rich person to enter the kingdom of heaven. Does that mean money is evil? Why or why not?
- The young man walks away grieving. Do you think he's grieving for his things? grieving that he won't enter the kingdom of heaven? grieving for some other reason? Explain.

Say: **Jesus' instructions aren't necessarily about what we have and don't have; more likely they're about how we view and use our possessions. If we put our things above our relationship with Jesus, then we're serving ourselves, not him. Jesus wants us to let go of anything we value over him. If we use possessions as tools to make an impact on the world, then we're living a Christlike life.**

MAKING A POSITIVE IMPACT IS A CHOICE

Ask:

- We don't actually know, but what choice do you think the rich young ruler made when he walked away from Jesus—and why?
- What sort of choices have you made to follow Jesus that maybe felt a little like the choice the rich young ruler had to make?
- As a follower of Jesus, what's the most significant choice you've made in the last few months?
- How have other people's positive, wise choices impacted your life? Be specific.
- How is choosing to follow Jesus unlike any other decision you can make in life?

Say: **Jesus gives us the freedom to live life and make choices, in the hopes that we choose him above all things. We face many choices, but the toughest choices often have the potential of making the greatest impact—in our lives and in other people's lives, too.**

TO MAKE THE GREATEST IMPACT, PUT YOUR FAITH INTO ACTION

Ask:

- What do you find most surprising about the way Jesus answers Peter's question in verse 27?
- What are some specific ways you currently put your faith into action?

- What are some excuses relative to following Jesus that you've made or seen that seem to hinder you from making an impact?
- What types of situations make it difficult to live out your faith, and how have you responded to those situations?

Say: **The rich young ruler believes in God and obeys his commandments. Yet Jesus tells him to give away all his possessions and spend it on the poor. Faith isn't just about believing; it's also about *being*. Being a Christ-follower has implications: Jesus calls us to have a positive impact on the world in ways that honor him.**

DIGGING DEEPER

Ask:

- **Read James 2:14-26. How can you summarize the main message of this Bible passage?**
- **Why is faith-in-action a powerful way to impact the world around you?**
- **Read Ephesians 2:8-10. What's the main point of these verses?**
- **In your own words, explain the difference between faith and actions. How are they the same? How are they different?**

PUTTING IT INTO PRACTICE

Ask:

- **For you, what's the most challenging thing we talked about today, and why?**
- **In what ways have you positively impacted the people around you?**
- **If you're facing a tough decision right now, consider it through the lens of what would honor Jesus the most—how does that impact the clarity of your choice?**
- **Salvation isn't dependent on our good deeds but on faith in Jesus through God's grace. What might you choose to do differently as a result of today's conversation?**

TEXTS & TWEETS

What's your most prized possession? Why is it so dear to you? Let's talk about it together.

What things do you hold onto tightly? What would be hard for you to let go of? Come share with the group.

Make texting your group easier. Consider using Simply Text. To try it FREE go to https://secure.symt.us/signup

THINGS TO REMEMBER

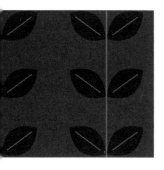

LESSON

PERSEVERE IN YOUR FAITH

Nº.09 BIBLE VERSES **James 1:1-18** James 1:19-27
Philippians 3:12-14

ACTIVITY

Say: **Sometimes the best strategy in life is to just persevere. We take what life throws at us, we work hard for a goal, we endure a series of difficult situations—whatever it is, we simply learn to practice perseverance. In many ways, that's like the process of training for an athletic competition, as we see in this clip.**

Play the clip.

Ask:

- **What do you think motivates Rocky to push through to the end?**
- **As you watched, how did this example of perseverance impact you? Why are examples of perseverance usually so powerful?**
- **In what ways is athletic training similar to spiritual growth?**

Say: **The spiritually beneficial way we respond to tough times isn't too different from the way athletes develop muscles or musicians master an instrument. Our response to the pressure of a difficult situation can increase our faith, our trust in Jesus, and our understanding of what it means to follow him.**

DIGGING IN

Have students take turns reading aloud James 1:1-18.

Say: **Let's dig deeper into James' message about persevering in our faith.**

GROWING IN FAITH IS A PROCESS

Ask:

- **Look closely at verses 2-4. In your own words, explain the process of growth James is describing here. What are some parallels or analogies to the process he describes?**
- **Why is perseverance important? How do you find the motivation to persevere?**

Things you need...

- ☐ A video clip from *Rocky*, from 1:30:30, as Rocky starts jogging, to 1:33:00, as Rocky stands at the top of the steps (Or use a training scene from another sports-related movie—and adjust the discussion questions, as necessary. For suggestions, see http://en.wikipedia.org/wiki/List_of_sports_films.)
- ☐ An Internet connection and a computer or tablet to display the video

BIBLE BACKGROUND

Read James 1:1-18.

James' writing style is pointed and intentional. He addresses several issues facing first-century Christians that remain relevant today, such as how to care for people on society's margins, how to persevere when life gets tough, and the importance of prayer.

Being a teenager can be difficult. Being a Christian teenager can be even harder. Parents and other adults expect young people to make choices that sometimes run contrary to what the culture says you should do. James acknowledges we all face situations that require perseverance, and he encourages us to focus on why choosing for God is worth it and how to do so.

Explore with your students how God wants us to respond to his love by the way we live. Emphasize grace and forgiveness, but also the impact of our actions. Being disciplined and making intentional choices to get sin out of our lives is biblical and important; these choices grow from our love of God because of his love for us!

For teenagers who don't yet follow Jesus, use this opportunity to share how God desires to give us full, complete, meaningful lives and how sin gets in the way of that.

- What kinds of "trials" do teenagers experience, and in what ways could these trials fuel spiritual growth?
- What do you think a "perfect and complete" faith looks like? Who do you know who has a mature Christian faith? What have you learned from them?
- Think about your life. When has Jesus taught you something powerful during or after a difficult situation or season? What was the experience, and what did you learn from it?

Say: James offers a pretty clear description of how our faith grows during tough times. Difficult situations test and challenge our faith, which means it has the opportunity to get stronger through our commitment and endurance. As our endurance increases, our faith becomes more and more mature—eventually reaching the point where it's "perfect and complete, needing nothing."

FIND STRENGTH THROUGH PRAYER

Ask:

- Read James 1:5-11. How does wisdom help us persevere through difficult situations?
- Talk about a time you faced a tough situation and prayed about it. How did Jesus respond to your prayer, and how did you grow spiritually through this experience?

Say: Prayer is simply communication with Jesus. It doesn't need to be fancy or long. It can simply be a real conversation. Prayer is an opportunity for us to share with Jesus our pain, stress, and gratefulness. And it's a chance for us to slow down and hear his voice—to consider how he's leading us, and to receive his counsel, encouragement, and care. He already knows what's happening in our lives, but when we tell him about our challenges, we build our relationship with him. When we pray, Jesus offers answers, wisdom, and strength.

PREPARE FOR PRESSURE POINTS

Ask:

- Read James 1:12-18. What are some misconceptions people have about the source and cause of temptation?
- Think about a recent temptation you faced. What was the source of it? What were you tempted to do—and did you do it? How did you handle the situation, and what did you learn from it?

Say: It's always good to remember that Jesus isn't the source of our temptation. Yes, he allows us to endure difficult situations. But he doesn't tempt us to sin or doubt or walk away from our faith. Those things come from the enemy, Satan, who wants nothing more than to knock people off-course spiritually.

DIGGING DEEPER

Ask:

- Read James 1:19-27. In this passage, James uses the metaphor of a mirror to talk about obedience. Using your own words, explain what he's communicating through this metaphor.
- When we experience a tough situation, we can either do the "right" thing, which is sometimes more difficult and takes more effort, or we can take the easy way out. What's the benefit of doing the right thing, and why is it often so tough to do? Be as personal and as specific as possible.
- Read Philippians 3:12-14. How would you describe the attitude Paul is talking about in these verses?
- What do you think is required of a Christian who perseveres to reach the "goal" Paul talks about? What steps, choices, or habits might be needed?
- For your own life and the challenges of this week, what do you need to forget? What do you need to focus on?

PUTTING IT INTO PRACTICE

Ask:

- What are some recent "tough times" you've had to endure? How did they challenge and stretch and grow you?
- What challenging time are you experiencing right now? What is Jesus teaching you?
- Talk about how you've cared for the "orphans" and "widows" in your world. What are some ways our group might do this?

Have students pair up and discuss these questions:

Ask:

- What's one way you're putting your faith into practice?
- How have you experienced Jesus strengthening you through prayer? How can I pray for you?
- What pressure points have caused you problems recently? How can we help each other?

Follow James' advice and have teenagers pray for wisdom for one another. Encourage students to call, text, or email each other during the week to pray for and encourage one another.

TEXTS & TWEETS

Facing something hard today? Join us to discover how to hold on to Jesus, who's holding on to you.

How do tough times teach priceless lessons? Share your thoughts and learn from others.

Make texting your group easier. Consider using Simply Text. To try it FREE go to https://secure.symt.us/signup

THINGS TO REMEMBER

LESSON

DISPLAY YOUR FAITH

N^{o.}10 BIBLE VERSES **James 2:14-26** 1 John 4:7-14
James 2:1-13

ACTIVITY

Read aloud the article as you eat the candy bar.

Ask:

- **What I just did is pretty hypocritical—what's the first thing that comes to mind when you hear the word "hypocrite"?**
- **Why is it so easy to hate hypocrisy? What makes it so distasteful?**
- **Nobody starts out wanting to be fake or two-faced. What do you think drives people to become hypocritical?**

DIGGING IN

Have students take turns reading aloud James 2:14-26.

Say: **So what does faith really look like? Let's examine what James teaches about this topic.**

TRUE FAITH LEADS TO ACTION

Say: **People in our culture have many different ideas about what it means to be "spiritual" or to have faith in God. James says it's not enough to just believe God exists—or even to believe that there's just one God. He says even demons believe this truth and "tremble" because of it.**

Ask:

- **If James says just believing God exists isn't enough for true faith, what does it take to have a living, genuine, true faith?**
- **What's the relationship between your faith and your deeds?**
- **James says faith without good works is dead. Does that mean good works can revitalize a person's dead or dying faith, or is something else required? Explain.**

Say: **It's important to remember that we don't "earn" salvation or Jesus' love. He loves you exactly the way you are, no matter what.**

Things you need...

- ☐ Print out the following article that focuses on the teenage obesity problem: http://tinyurl.com/jh944wu
- ☐ A candy bar

BIBLE BACKGROUND

Read James 2.

As Christians, we have the opportunity and the enthusiasm to display our faith through our actions. It's worth remembering that the first Christians didn't ask to be called "Christians." They got that name from people who observed their actions as Christ-followers. It was obvious by the way these Christians lived that they loved and followed Jesus.

The Bible clearly teaches that salvation comes through faith in Jesus, not through works. We can't earn our way to heaven, we can't deserve grace, and we can't make ourselves good enough to stand in God's perfect presence.

Many kinds of faith and belief exist—everything from weak opinions to strong convictions. James clearly defines the kind of faith a Christian who has gone all-in with Jesus has: one that translates into action. He makes it very simple and clear: Faith without deeds is dead.

Challenge teenagers to take their faith outside the church doors by how they treat peers, respond to stressful situations, interact with authority figures, and care for people in need. Opportunities to show Jesus' love are as endless as Jesus' love itself.

And you can never be "good enough" to earn salvation. It's a free gift from Jesus that has nothing to do with how good or bad you are. However, when we love Jesus and choose to follow him, he calls us to respond and put our faith into action. Our love for Jesus and for others is what leads to action.

TRUE FAITH REJECTS PREJUDICE

Say: **It's natural to spend time with a best friend, do favors for others on a sports team, buy birthday gifts for family members, and encourage classmates we like. But the challenge James presents in the first part of chapter 2 is for Christians to demonstrate faith by the way we love all people—especially those who might be considered "different" or "outcasts."**

Ask:

- **How do you define the word "prejudice"? How is this word connected to concepts such as discrimination, injustice, racism, and hatred?**
- **Read James 2:1-13. Which of the examples of prejudice James mentions remain with us today, and why? Give some examples of how you've seen or experienced these prejudices.**
- **In your world, which groups of people are often the targets of prejudice, and which groups often receive special attention?**

DIGGING DEEPER

- **Read 1 John 4:7-14. How would you summarize what John writes about the way Christians are called to treat each other?**
- **When do you find it easy to follow this kind of advice? When do you find it difficult to follow this kind of advice? Explain.**

PUTTING IT INTO PRACTICE

Ask:

- **Name one person who's easy for you to love and care for. What recent actions show that you love and care for this person?**
- **Without naming anyone, think about people in your life who are harder to love and care for (and if you're sitting next to one, don't poke them!). What have you tried to do to show that you love that person anyway?**
- **James uses Abraham and Rahab as examples of people whose faith and actions are connected. What people in your life might serve as role models as you take steps to put your faith in action in greater ways? What can you learn from these individuals?**

- What's one way you can respond to Jesus' love and do something this week that reflects your faith? When will you do this? And how can we encourage each other in this step of faith?

THINGS TO REMEMBER

TEXTS & TWEETS

Do your actions point people to Jesus? Come find out how to keep your faith alive and growing.

What's the difference between an opinion and a conviction? Can't wait to see you for a great conversation.

Make texting your group easier. Consider using Simply Text. To try it FREE go to https://secure.symt.us/signup

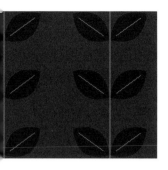

LESSON

WATCH YOUR WORDS

NO.11

BIBLE VERSES **James 3:1-12** James 3:13-18
Ephesians 4:29

ACTIVITY

Say: **Ever had one of those moments when you didn't really know what to say? You knew you needed to say something, but you just couldn't find the right words. That's what happens in this scene from** *As Good As It Gets,* **as Melvin struggles to find the right words to say to Carol after insulting her dress.**

Play the clip.

Ask:

- **Think of a time you were encouraged by what someone else said about you. How did those words impact you?**
- **Think of a time you were hurt by words someone spoke, either to your face or behind your back. How did those words impact you?**
- **Why can it be so tough for us to compliment other people—and avoid making negative statements?**
- **Why do you think Jesus cares so much about the words we speak and write?**

Say: **Our words are remarkable things. It's no exaggeration to say we can destroy a person with what we say or write—or we can help lift that person to new heights. That's why Jesus cares so much about our words. They're a reflection of whether we love the people around us or are focused on just our own selfish desires. The good news is that we can grow and mature in this area.**

DIGGING IN

Have students take turns reading aloud James 3:1-12.

Say: **Let's see what James says about this common, universal struggle to control our tongue and watch our words.**

Things you need...

- ☐ A video clip from *As Good As It Gets,* from 1:37:30, as Melvin sits, to 1:40:30, as Melvin says, "You make me want to be a better man."
- ☐ An Internet connection and a computer or tablet to display the video

BIBLE BACKGROUND

Read James 3.

Verses 1-12 are the primary verses for the lesson, but some of the focus also is on verses 13-18.

James understands the importance and impact of words. He compares the power of speech to a rudder guiding an entire ship. He reminds us that words can destroy, just like a small spark starts a fire. The call to tame the tongue is a relevant message for teenagers.

Words are powerful. A simple statement can make or ruin someone's day. With technology, we can instantly share words in emails, texts, posts, instant messages, and other conversations—often without much thought. Few sentences have the power of "I love you" or the disappointment of "No, I'm not interested." A seemingly innocent joke or comment can make someone feel awkward and worthless. At the same time, an encouraging letter or comment may restore confidence.

It's easy to slip into gossip, critical comments, sarcasm, or blatant attacks. It's easy to keep our words superficial or talk to make conversation rather than to make a difference.

YOUR WORDS CAN BUILD UP OR TEAR DOWN

Ask:

- **What are some ways our words can negatively affect the people around us?** (gossip, dissension, tone of voice, etc.)
- **Look at verses 9-12. Has this happened to you before? You worship Jesus at church or in youth group or during devotions, and then you turn around and speak something hurtful or hateful. Maybe those words really did feel bitter or salty as you spoke them. Why do we do this?**
- **How do negative or critical words—whether we speak them about others or receive them ourselves—impact the way we see ourselves?**
- **Do our attitudes shape our words, or do our words shape our attitudes? Explain.**

Say: **Most words and conversations aren't neutral. We're either honoring or dishonoring other people—and Jesus. That's why it's important to learn to be intentional about our words. Am I about to honor or dishonor someone? Am I about to build someone up or tear someone down? Am I about to respect or demean that person? Pausing to reconnect with Jesus, asking for his Spirit to guide you, before you speak or write something can help you choose a better path.**

WORDS PRODUCE UNCONTROLLABLE RESULTS

Ask:

- **Look at verses 3-12. Why do you think James chooses these particular analogies—a horse, a ship, a fire, and a fountain—to describe the power of our words?**
- **Describe a time when something you said was misunderstood. What did you learn? How would you say it differently?**

Say: **After you say something, you can't bring it back. It's been spoken, and it's been heard. You can ask for forgiveness after speaking or writing hurtful words, but you can't completely erase the experience for the person who heard or read your words.**

WISDOM CAN HELP US CONTROL OUR WORDS

Ask:

- **What is the nature of wisdom? What does it look like to use wisdom with your words?**
- **Read James 3:13-18. What are some of the personal boundaries a wise person sets up before they speak?**
- **When is it necessary to use negative words? Explain.**

Say: **Verses 13-18 offer insight about the relationship between our words and our spiritual maturity. James' examples reflect situations where words will either heal or harm. Bitter jealousy and selfish ambition are reflected in our words through boasting and lying. The opposite is also true: Mercy, sincerity, gentleness, and a willingness to yield to others are evidenced through the atmosphere of peace that our words create. We can ask Jesus for wisdom in the words we choose and use.**

DIGGING DEEPER

Ask:

- **Why do you think James spends so much time in his letter talking about the power of words?**
- **Verse 18 says, "Peacemakers will plant seeds of peace and reap a harvest of righteousness." What are some ways your words have been "seeds of peace"?**
- **What might James write or say to your generation about the power of words? What are some unique challenges and opportunities young people now face?**

Say: **Close your eyes for a moment, and think about a time when you felt wounded by another person's words. I won't ask for details; just think about how those words hurt and affected you.** (Pause.) **Now think about a time when another person's words provided strength, encouragement, and joy. The words were almost like a treasure or healing medicine at that particular moment.** (Pause.) **Now open your eyes.**

Ask:

- **Those two memories brought different sets of emotions, right? Without giving details, tell why the words—either the negative or positive ones—were so powerful.**
- **No one likes to receive negative words, yet we all struggle to not use them against other people. How could this exercise help you the next time you're about to criticize, slam, or talk negatively about someone? How might it help you look for more opportunities to share positive words with others?**

PUTTING IT INTO PRACTICE

Have students pair up to discuss these questions:

Ask:

- **What are the biggest temptations you face with your words? Do you tend to gossip about others? Do you struggle with**

TEXTS & TWEETS

What friend have you encouraged today? Join us as we study the book of James.

What did you talk about with your friends today? Come hear how much our words matter.

Make texting your group easier. Consider using Simply Text. To try it FREE go to https://secure.symt.us/signup

making fun of people? Do you keep silent when you could be encouraging or standing up for someone?

- How have you grown—or struggled—in this area during the past few years?
- Read Ephesians 4:29. What will it take to reach the place where "everything" we say is "good and helpful"? What one step can we each take this week to move closer to that kind of Christlike maturity?

Challenge students to email or text you afterward with one area where they're struggling—or have pairs text each other. If teenagers struggle with gossip, challenge them to work together on this. If most of the gossip happens at lunch, suggest they sit someplace different so they can break the habit. If it occurs mainly through texts or social media, encourage them to not type anything about anyone else for the week and put a note on their phones or computers to remember this commitment.

THINGS TO REMEMBER

ACTIVITY

Give kids each a small square of aluminum foil and ask them to use it like a mirror, with the shiny side facing them. Have them hold the foil so their face fills the entire square, then ask them to stare at their own face as you begin...

Say: **Imagine going through your entire day without a single concern for another person. Every minute of every hour is all about you. Everyone around you has to focus every ounce of energy on pleasing and satisfying you! It'd be something like what you're experiencing right now—your face is the only one you can see. Of course, that's fine for a little bit, but what about... all the time? I'll be quiet for a minute while you just stare at yourself. Please also be quiet during the next 60 seconds.** (Pause for one minute.)

Ask:

- **What would it be like to live this way—focused on yourself all the time?**
- **At first, you might enjoy that kind of attention, but over time, what would that kind of life be like?**
- **If everything in the world revolved around you, how would that change the way you interact with Jesus?**
- **Of course, we don't go to this extreme, but how does this experience remind you of the way we live sometimes?**

Say: **Sometimes we dream about what it would be like if the entire world revolved around us, but that isn't how Jesus calls us to live. Our selfish sins create barriers and undermine healthy relationships with Jesus and other people. But he can help us grow and change in these areas, allowing us to grow more deeply into an other-centered mindset.**

Things you need...

☐ A small square of aluminum foil for each person

BIBLE BACKGROUND

Read James 4:1-17.

James continues to give direct advice for Christians. Chapter 4 reveals what gets in the way in our relationship with God—and we know from experience how these things also affect our relationships with other people. James addresses jealousy, pride, judgment, and boasting—and their destructive consequences. This Bible passage offers a reminder of how God brings healing and freedom from those things through Jesus.

We become jealous when we see other people succeeding in ways we want to succeed or acquiring things we desire. Pride is the sense that we're superior or perfect or better than others. It often leads to a feeling of judgment toward others, especially people who are poor, less talented, or seemingly less blessed. And boasting is the decision to forget God's role in our lives; we think we've accomplished things on our own.

All these selfish conditions are common among teenagers, and they all hurt relationships. Fortunately, students can learn how to avoid or combat these attitudes. Find ways to encourage the selfless behavior and attitudes you've observed. Focus on positive, Jesus-honoring traits, and discuss how selfless actions help us battle against selfishness.

DIGGING IN

Have students take turns reading aloud James 4:1-17.

Say: **I think it's true that we all want healthy, meaningful relationships, so let's see what we can learn from James about protecting these relationships.**

JEALOUSY IS A POISON

Ask:

- **Read verses 1-3. How have fights or quarrels undermined healthy relationships in your life?**
- **If Christians are called and equipped to live differently, why do we sometimes have the same kinds of fights and quarrels with people?**
- **Which of the relationship problems James mentions do you encounter or observe on a regular basis?**
- **How does jealousy affect your relationship with Jesus? How does it affect your relationships with other people?**

Say: **We sometimes get annoyed by people who get things we want. Jesus desires to bless us in different ways—sometimes not in the ways we think are best for us. But instead of praying about it and talking to the one who loves us and desires the best for us, we let jealousy toward others smolder inside. Jesus is all about relationships, and jealousy affects our human relationships and our relationship with him. But we can ask Jesus for help when we feel jealous or envious.**

SURRENDER AND HUMILITY PROVIDE AN ANTIDOTE

Ask:

- **Read verses 4-12. In one sentence, how would you summarize James' message here?**
- **How can pride affect your relationship with Jesus? How does it affect your relationships with other people?**
- **Why is it so easy to judge and evaluate others? Why are we so quick to judge others when we hate to be judged ourselves?**
- **How can judgment affect your relationship with Jesus? How can it affect your relationships with other people?**
- **If a selfish perspective on life is like a poison, what are some of the antidotes?**

Say: **All of us battle with pride. But when we submit to Jesus out of trust and love, he offers freedom and gives us a weapon in the battle against sin. James tells us that Jesus will lift us up when we're humble. We can't escape from sin on our own; we need Jesus.**

AVOID THE TRAP OF OVERCONFIDENCE

Ask:

- **Read verses 13-17. What's the dividing line between healthy confidence and overconfidence? When have you crossed it?**
- **How can overconfidence affect your relationship with Jesus? How does it affect your relationships with other people?**

Say: James reminds us that only God knows what will happen in the future. God is master and creator of the universe, and James reminds us to take on a humble, dependent attitude. It's not sinful to have confidence, but boasting about the idea that we have God's knowledge and power is sinful.

DIGGING DEEPER

Ask:

- **How do you define the word "humble"? Who has it?**
- **Read Philippians 2:3-11. What can we learn from Jesus' humility? What has helped you most in your practice of humility?**
- **How can a Christian be both humble and confident?**
- **How would you describe our culture's attitude toward humility? What are some examples to back up your opinion?**
- **Can you have a healthy relationship with Jesus but unhealthy relationships with other people? Why or why not? Can you have an unhealthy relationship with Jesus but healthy relationships with other people? Why or why not?**
- **What do you think it means that the Spirit envies intensely (see James 4:5)? What does this say about Jesus' character?**

PUTTING IT INTO PRACTICE

Say: **So far in this lesson, we've talked about jealousy, pride, judgment, and overconfidence—four selfish traits that can affect our relationships with Jesus and other people. What are the remedies? How do we protect our relationships against sin? Find a partner and discuss these questions together.**

Ask:

- **Pick one of the four areas where you feel you're struggling the most. In your own heart, where do you think this is coming from?**
- **What verse or phrase from today's lesson gives you some practical help to handle this issue?** (Note: It may help to reread the chapter.)
- **How can we help each other as we grow in these areas? What action steps can we take together?**

TEXTS & TWEETS

What's the #1 thing that keeps your friendships from going to the next level? Can't wait to see you soon for a great discussion.

How can you have better relationships? Come find out— and invite a friend along!

Make texting your group easier. Consider using Simply Text. To try it FREE go to https://secure.symt.us/signup

THINGS TO REMEMBER

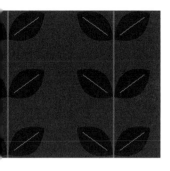

ACTIVITY

Ask a student to come up front, then have that person open his or her arms wide with palms facing up. Then ask kids, one by one, to come up and begin making a stack of objects on both of the volunteer's palms. The idea is to progressively put more weight on his or her outstretched arms—challenge the volunteer to keep his or her arms stretched out as long as possible. When he or she can't take any more weight, ask kids to quickly remove objects from the stacks they've built, one by one.

Ask the volunteer:

- **What was going through your mind and heart during this activity? Explain.**
- **What helped you to persevere, and what did you tell yourself as this challenge got harder?**

Ask the group:

- **What were you feeling as you added to the weight on our volunteer's arms? when you took weight off?**

Say: **Like this challenge, life requires courage, strength, and stamina. It's easy to feel like we're not up to the challenge, and we often feel like we need someone to take some of the weight off. In Matthew 11 Jesus tells us: "Come to me, all of you who are weary and carry heavy burdens, and I will give you rest. Take my yoke upon you. Let me teach you, because I am humble and gentle at heart, and you will find rest for your souls. For my yoke is easy to bear, and the burden I give you is light." Let's explore what a perseverant life looks like...**

DIGGING IN

Have students take turns reading aloud James 5:1-20.

Things you need...

- ☐ Objects of various weight to put in someone's hands

BIBLE BACKGROUND

Read James 5:1-20.

In the final chapter of this book, James continues his direct approach about Christian living. Repeating a theme from the beginning of the letter (1:9-11), he talks about how we treat people who are poor. He's particularly harsh on rich oppressors, warning that God genuinely cares how we use our money. James also discusses endurance, the power of our words, and the importance of protecting our relationships. And he tackles the topics of prayer and confession, offering new challenges for readers.

TAKING ADVANTAGE OF OTHERS HAS ITS DISADVANTAGES

Say: It can be easy to skip over verses 1-6, because few of us qualify as "rich oppressors." After all, when was the last time you failed to pay an employee? But this passage still has some meaning for our lives.

Ask:

- God obviously opposes oppression. Why do you think people take advantage of others? What's at the heart of this issue?
- Do you ever treat things as more important than people? If you feel comfortable, explain what this looks like in your life.
- How do you define "self-indulgence"? When does legitimate joy cross the line into self-indulgence? What insights from this Bible passage might help answer this question?

PATIENCE ISN'T EASY TO DEVELOP

Ask:

- How do you develop patience? What kinds of situations or experiences are most effective at creating patience in your life?
- What's the link between patience and spiritual growth?
- In verses 10-11, James says Christians can find encouragement by remembering men and women who persevered, even when their faith was challenged. How has learning about the stories of other Christians helped you develop patience and perseverance?

Say: Most people want to be patient but don't enjoy going through the tough experiences that help us *become* patient. Some people have an incredible ability to be patient in the middle of stressful situations. But for most of us, it's a growth process. Patience is a fruit of the Spirit, so regularly pray for Jesus to help you grow in this area.

PRAY FOR EACH OTHER ON THE JOURNEY

Say: When we pray—whether aloud as a group or individually—it's important to be honest with Jesus. I think we all "know" that prayer is essential to spiritual growth, but sometimes we overlook the value of praying for each other and with each other.

Ask:

- In verses 13-20, James talks about praying for people when they're sick, confessing sins to each other, and praying for Christians to be restored. What are some other benefits of Christians praying for each other?
- What's the connection between confessing our sins to each other and praying for each other?

- How does praying for and with a friend strengthen your friendship? How does this kind of prayer help you grow spiritually and take greater ownership of your faith?

DIGGING DEEPER

Ask:
- After reading James 5, are you optimistic or pessimistic? Why?
- Read James 5:12. What's James' main idea in this verse?
- In verse 9, James talks about Christians "grumbling" about each other. What does he mean? How does grumbling affect our relationships with one another?
- Read Matthew 6:9-13. What elements of Jesus' instructions on prayer are similar to what James writes in chapter 5?

PUTTING IT INTO PRACTICE

Ask:
- How are you honoring Jesus in the challenges you're facing?
- How do you display love for the "poor" and "needy" in your life?
- Let's do a tongue check: Are you gossiping? insulting? criticizing? Or are you focusing more on encouraging others?
- How is your prayer life? Who are you praying for? How have you praised Jesus today? Are you confessing your sins?
- Where do you want to be encouraged in these areas?

THINGS TO REMEMBER

TEXTS & TWEETS

When is it tough for you to be patient? How does that impact your faith and friendships? Be sure to join us this week.

How is your spiritual journey going? Come out for some encouragement and challenge.

Make texting your group easier. Consider using Simply Text. To try it FREE go to https://secure.symt.us/signup

13 ESSENTIAL LESSONS FROM THE OLD TESTAMENT

If you liked doing these lessons from the New Testament, then you'll love the next in the series. Available online and at your local Christian bookstore.

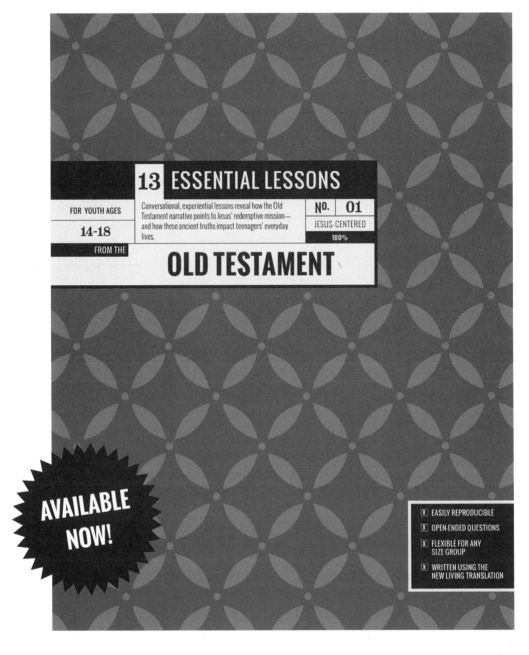

ISBN 978-1-4707-4289-8